MALVOLIO

Betty Shamieh

BROADWAY PLAY PUBLISHING INC
New York
www.broadwayplaypublishing.com
info@broadwayplaypublishing.com

MALVOLIO
© Copyright 2024 Betty Shamieh

Cover photo by Richard Termine

First edition: August 2024
I S B N: 979-8-88856-028-0

Book design: Marie Donovan
Page make-up: Adobe InDesign
Typeface: Palatino

For my son
Alexander
who is my biggest blessing and greatest inspiration

MALVOLIO has its world premiere at the Richard Rodgers Amphitheatre in Marcus Garvey Park as part of the Classical Theatre of Harlem's Annual Uptown Shakespeare in the Park series in New York, NY (Ty Jones, Producing Artistic Director; Michael Windham, General Manager) on 8 July 2023. The cast and creative contributors were:

MALVOLIO .... Allen Gilmore
VOLINA .... Kineta Kunutu
VIOLA ....Perri Gaffney
ORSINO ....René Thorton
OLIVIA ....Stephanie Berry
SEBASTIAN ....Nathan M Ramsey
MARIA..Paula Galloway
SIR TOBY BELCH ....David Ryan Smith
FOOL .... Matthew J Harris
KING CHADLIO ....John-Andrew Morrison
PRINCE FURTADO...JD Mollison
CURIOUS .... Collin McConnell
VALENTIN.. Tony Macht
FATHER TOPAS ....CB Murray
NURSE .... Marjorie Johnson

Ensemble ....Marcus Byers, Jr, John DeFilippo,
Byrnlie Helmich, Valériane Louisy,
Al-Nisa Petty, Duane Shabazz,
Jonathan McClinton Smith, Timothy Wilson

Co-Directors.................................... Ian Belknap & Ty Jones
Lighting Designer .... Alan C Edwards
Choreographer.......................................Dell Howlett
Set Designers ....Christopher & Justin Swader
Sound Designer ....Frederick Kennedy
Costume Designer......................................Celeste Jennings
Video Designer........................Zavier Augustus Lee Taylor
Production Stage Manager..............................Jessica Forella
Hair & Makeup Designer ....Earon Nealey
Stage Manager ....Mary Kate Baughman

CHARACTERS & SETTING

MALVOLIO, *a general and former servant to* OLIVIA
VOLINA, *daughter of* ORSINO *and* VIOLA
VIOLA, *Duchess of Illyria, married to* ORSINO
ORSINO, *Duke of Illyria, married to* VIOLA
OLIVIA, *a countess, married to* SEBASTIAN
SEBASTIAN, VIOLA'*s twin brother, married to* OLIVIA
MARIA, OLIVIA'*s former servant, now married to* SIR TOBY
SIR TOBY BELCH, OLIVIA'*s cousin*
FOOL, *a court jester (also called Feste)*
KING CHADLIO, *King of Illyria*
PRINCE FURTADO, KING'*s son*
CURIOUS/VALENTIN, *servants (these parts can be doubled)*
FATHER TOPAS, *a priest*
NURSE, VOLINA'*s nursemaid*

Casting requirements: 14 actors

*Place: The ancient region of Illyria and other island nations
on the Eastern coast of the Adriatic Sea.*

Time: Twenty years after TWELFTH NIGHT *ends*

Scene 1

(Lights up on MALVOLIO. *He is wearing battle gear with cross-gartered yellow stockings. He snaps his fingers. There is the sound of military drumming.)*

MALVOLIO:
Legion of the Cross Gartered!
Bravest of our Brave King's Men!
Music in wartime makes men machines.
Beat on!
Brothers, the war you don't start
is the one you most need to win.
Take no prisoners. Show no mercy.
Go! Fight! Kill!

(Lights shift to a bedroom in Illyria.)

NURSE:
Sit!
We only have four hours to ready you for your party,
Volina.

VOLINA:
Four hours is plenty, Nurse.

NURSE:
Your father has invited all the notables of Illyria.
Sit.

VOLINA:
The only notables of Illyria
are the ones who are off fighting to defend Illyria.
I can't party while our soldiers are at war.

NURSE:
Dear girl,
war might be waging.
No one knows it better than I.
My son is among the soldiers.
If I can still smile,
so must you, Volina,
especially on your birthday.
Sit.

VOLINA:
It seems wrong somehow.
Selfish. All of Illyria is selfish.

NURSE:
Our home may be far from heaven.
Sure, there is war and famine.
Did you cause it? No.
Can you end it? No.
Forget the woes of a world you can't change,
you can't do more than you can.

VOLINA:
(*Aside*) Maybe. But, I certainly can do more than I'm
doing now.
Can I do as my mother, Viola, once did long ago?
She landed on our island—a stranger to all—and
dressed as a boy.
Can I disguise myself as male too?
To enlist in our army where women soldiers are not
welcome?
To fight for our people?
To matter?

(*The lights shift to* VIOLA *and* ORSINO'*s room.*)

VIOLA:
Come! Orsino, we have to tell our daughter tonight.

ORSINO:
Fine, but after the party is over.

It's a great honor that King Chadlio wants her to marry
his only son.

VIOLA:
She may not see it that way.
What if Volina refuses?

ORSINO:
He's the crown prince!
No woman can withstand wooing
from a crown prince
who could make her a queen.

VIOLA:
The things you say about women
are so—

ORSINO:
So?

VIOLA:
Clearly words that a man would think about a woman.

ORSINO:
Oh, for heaven's sake, Cesario!
I mean, Olivia.
I mean, Wife.
Dearest, I will stick with calling you wife.

VIOLA:
And what a husband you turned out to be!

ORSINO:
Wife, I'm sorry.
It was only one time.

VIOLA:
One time was enough!
My poor dear brother, Sebastian!
What luck!
To survive a shipwreck
only to drown in a shipwreck,
the very next time he goes out to sea.

And to have you, Orsino,
bed his widow within the fortnight.

ORSINO:
A fortnight is a long time.
You knew I was in love with Olivia.
No one knew it more than you.
Yet, you married me anyway.
Wife, let's go greet our guests.

VIOLA:
Let's.

Scene 2

(A royal chamber. KING is seated. MALVOLIO enters and bows before him.)

KING:
Rise! We were told you requested an audience with us,
Soldier.
We have heard much of your bravery on the battlefield.

MALVOLIO:
To be fair, Your Highness.
I'm only as brave as the men I command.
My legion is fearless.
We have almost driven out the Barbarian nation for
good.
With enough support, I believe we can win this war.

KING:
Well, any war can be won with enough support.
The question is whether we can afford it.
Your request for provisions has been noted.
But, first, we want to know more of you.

MALVOLIO:
I am called General Malvolio, Leader of the Legion of

the Cross-Gartered.
and I left my home, Illyria, to enlist when—

KING:
You're from Illyria!
Of all the island-nations I rule over, Illyria is my most
beloved.
For the women are prettiest there, no?
IF I had my druthers,
I would not have wed any woman who was not an
Illyrian.
But, the problem with ruling a constellation of islands
is that everyone is always trying to secede.
You know how that is. Such a pain.

MALVOLIO:
Actually, I don't.

KING:
Long ago, an ancestor of mine made a decree,
that the crown prince must marry from one of the
islands we rule
and it would rotate every generation. So, I had to
marry from Dalmatia
and you know what dogs those women are.

MALVOLIO:
Um—

KING:
That's all to say,
I'm fond of your island.
I like Illyria as well as you do.

MALVOLIO:
You could only like Illyria as I like Illyria
if you don't like Illyria at all.
I joined your army to escape there.
Have you never heard the story of Malvolio,
the former steward to Countess Olivia?

KING:
No.

MALVOLIO:
Really?
I thought I was famous.

KING:
I am a busy man.

MALVOLIO:
Of course.
I was once unfairly treated in Olivia's house.
My humiliation made me reckless.
Reckless men make great soldiers.
When I rose to the rank of general,
I surrounded myself with men like me,
who care not if they live or die.
It is they who make up the Legion of the Cross-
Gartered,
and they that Your Highness should honor as well as I.

KING:
That sounds expensive.
I like you, Morosio.

MALVOLIO:
It's Malvolio.

KING:
Of course. Malvolio.
It's a bit hard to remember.
Do you mind if I call you Morosio?

MALVOLIO:
I can refuse you no request, Your Highness.

KING:
No, that's too much. I'm always asking too much.
My father was always reminding me
that lesser people don't like it when you rename them.
My son and heir, Prince Furtado, could learn much

from you.
He is itching to learn the art of warfare, as every prince
should.
Or at least, I am itching he learn the art of something.
Before you return to the battlefield,
dine with us tonight.

MALVOLIO:
What an honor, Your Highness.

(*Lights shift to* VOLINA. NURSE *is putting on her makeup.*)

VOLINA:
What a waste of time grooming is.

NURSE:
Yes, it must be such hard work for you.

VOLINA: (*Speaking to her image in a mirror*)
What enemy or friend is this?
My body,
the borrowed envelope that holds my spirit,
the meat of me,
that is different from my mind that asks,

'Are you a beast
that must be beat into submission?
Fed less than it desires?
A thing to be tamed?

Or are you an orphan I chanced upon?
A mewing, hungry, helpless, abandoned thing
I must save?'

How can my mind and body
not be at war,
when my mind knows
my body
is the only thing my world regards?

(FOOL *appears at the window.*)

FOOL:
Enough of that!

Try being hungry.
You learn quick if your body or mind is boss then.

VOLINA:
True. How are you, Feste?

FOOL:
Obviously better than you.
Why so dreary?
On your birthday, of all days.

VOLINA:
A rose doesn't choose
the color of its bloom.

FOOL:
Well, luckily, you are no rose.
As far as I can tell, you are a girl.

NURSE:
A girl who is
full of youth, beauty, rank, and property,
who looks like an angel
but speaks only of hell.

FOOL:
There are a thousand women
who would trade places with you.

VOLINA:
And not one man.

FOOL:
I would trade places with you in a heartbeat.
To be fed all I wanted and to be the pet of this
household.

VOLINA:
Yes, I am too well petted.

NURSE:
I heard you joined the monastery, Fool.
Why?

FOOL:
Because praying for my daily bread
was the only way I could find any bread at all.
No one will feed a fool during wartime
when it's clear
everyone has a fool in their family.

NURSE:
What do you mean?

FOOL:
Everyone has a soldier in their family,
willing to die at the hands of a Barbarian
because a king asks it of them.

NURSE:
Bite your tongue off.
My son is among the soldiers.

VOLINA:
If you speak treason,
I'll report you to the King.

FOOL:
And if you report me to the King—

VOLINA:
What?

FOOL:
I'll be quite upset.
Don't be angry, Nurse.
May your son live long, marry well, and make you
many grandsons who you can also delight in
donating to the war effort.
Can my father come to the party too?

VOLINA:
Your father?

(FATHER TOPAS *appears on the balcony. He's very old.*)

NURSE:
It's you. Father Topas! Hello, O Most Valiant of Men!
Don't you recognize me?

FOOL:
You know my father?

NURSE:
Yes, long ago. He knew me too. Very well.

FOOL:
Well, he doesn't know you now.
He doesn't know anyone.
He's lost his memory.
I went to the monastery in part to care for him.
Even though he never acknowledged me as his son,
I still like him. I'm foolish like that.
Volina, let us come to your feast and we'll pray for you
every day.

VOLINA:
I thought you said your father had no memory.

FOOL:
I'll remind him.
Maiden, you want to be brave, noble, wonderful and
admired.

VOLINA:
Fool, I long to live admirably, not be admired.

FOOL:
Want the secret of how to be both?

VOLINA:
Sure.

FOOL:
Change the colors of your petals.
Smile!
And make sure I get ale.

VOLINA:
Ale is forbidden to us during wartime.
The medics need it to ease the pain of wounded
soldiers.
My father would never allow it in our house.

(VIOLA *calls from off-stage.*)

VIOLA:
Volina!

ORSINO:
Your godmother Olivia has come. Come eat with us.

VOLINA:
I will not sit at a table and smile during wartime.
Dine without me!

ORSINO:
But it's your birthday, Daughter.

VOLINA: *(Under her breath)*
Doesn't stop you from flirting with Aunt Olivia,
Father.
(To FOOL*)*
If I invite you, Feste,
my parents will hate it.
I'm coming! And I've brought a few guests of my own!

(VOLINA *enters the dining space, where her family is
gathered.* FOOL *and* FATHER TOPAS *follow her.*)

ORSINO:
Welcome, my guests! Fine folks and good friends all!
Wait! You have invited the Fool to dine?

VOLINA:
Yes.

ALL: *(Except* VOLINA *and* FOOL*)*
Hooray!

OLIVIA:
It's been so long since I've seen you, Fool.

FOOL:
Do not slander me.
I'm not married.

OLIVIA:
Slander you?

FOOL:
You married. I did not.
That makes you the fool.

ORSINO:
You are right. It is we who are the fools.

VIOLA:
Thanks!

OLIVIA:
Dear goddaughter, I heard some good news about—

VIOLA:
Nothing! You have heard nothing
about my daughter.

OLIVIA:
I did not mean to offend you.
It was good of you to invite me.

VIOLA:
My husband did the inviting.
Many women find him very inviting.
It is you who chose whether or not to accept.

OLIVIA:
Forgive me. I assumed the invitation came from you,
too,
for the sake of appearances,
lest there'll be gossip if I don't attend my
goddaughter's feast.
I'll go.

VIOLA:
And make a scene of leaving early after speaking with

me?
Oh no! O-livia! O False Sister!
You came. You will eat cake.
After my daughter is safely married to a man so
powerful,
that the venom of wagging tongues can never touch
her,
stop your ears! Tear out your eyes! Hobble your own
feet
before you dare approach this house again.

(*SIR* TOBY *and* MARIA *enter.*)

VOLINA:
You are invited, Toby?

MARIA:
Why wouldn't my husband be invited? We're family!

TOBY:
Yes, family! And I've brought ale.

VOLINA:
Ale is supposed to be rationed, Toby.
How can you forget we are at war?

ORSINO:
It's not a party without ale.

VOLINA:
Father!

ORSINO:
I'm not going to go out of my way to procure ale.
That's against the law.
But, if it happens to find its way to my table,
why not?
Before we begin,
Father Topas, would you like to say a prayer?

FATHER TOPAS:
Yes, Your Highness.

ORSINO:
I'm no King. I'm just a Duke.

FATHER TOPAS:
Yes, Your Highness.

ORSINO:
So that means Your Grace is fine.

FATHER TOPAS:
Yes, Your Highness.

FOOL:
My father says "Yes, Your Highness"
to everything and everyone.
It's a carry-over from some shard of a
fragment of a memory. I'll do it for him.
Let us pray.

Blessed are the blessed,
Because being blessed is so much damn fun.

Blessed are those who never play by the rules,
they understand life is no game.

Blessed are those who need no other proof there is a
God
than that we can tune our own instruments and play
solo.

Blessed are the women,
Because they can be both ravishing and ravished at the
same time.

Blessed are the kings who all look to the one same sun,
whose realms they populate with other kinds of sons,
usually fiery but hardly ever bright,
also known as
royal bastards.

Amen.

VOLINA:
Who are you to speak such blasphemy?

TOBY:
Who wants the first drink?

(Music starts up and all except VOLINA *dance.)*

VOLINA:
Our men are dying and you all dance.
Our soldiers are starving
and you eat cake and ale.
Toby must pay for polluting my family,
tempting them with provisions stolen from our
suffering soldiers.
I'll go to the King and tell him
his people are not abiding by the war rations!
While they revel, I won't be missed.
Tonight I will steal my mother's clothing,
that she wore when she disguised herself as a boy long
ago.
I'll sneak out to board the next boat
to tell the king all!

Scene 3

(Onstage are the PRINCE *and the* KING.*)*

KING:
Son, tonight you will break bread with a war hero.
Would that you could learn a few lessons from him!
He is saving our territory from the Barbarians.

PRINCE:
So I've heard. Is he fun? Does he swallow swords?
Juggle knives?

KING:
Are you drunk?

PRINCE:
Only slightly.

*(*MALVOLIO *enters and bows.)*

PRINCE:
You are Malvolio?
You are the leader of the legion of legions,
the battalion of the infamous Cross-Gartered?
You?

MALVOLIO:
At your service, Sire.

PRINCE:
It must be admitted you are ordinary.

KING:
But a man of extraordinary courage.
A war hero.
In fact, I'm going to make you a knight.

MALVOLIO:
Thank you, Your Highness.
(*Aside*)
Is this not a sign that greatness is being thrust upon
me?
Surely, becoming a knight will bring me one step closer
to avenging myself for the great humiliation
I suffered in Olivia's household long ago.

(MALVOLIO *bows before him. The* KING *is surprised.*)

MALVOLIO:
I swear to be faithful to My King and all his heirs.
I swear to always defend a lady.
I swear to be on time for battles—

KING:
Wait. You already know the oaths?

MALVOLIO:
I had a mother who believed I was destined for great
things.
She made me memorize the oaths as a boy.

PRINCE:
Okay, but we usually knight people after dinner.

KING:
Never mind. No time like the present.
In our name, you are knighted Sir Mongolio.

PRINCE:
Malvolio, Father.
His name is Malvolio.

KING:
That's what I said.
Arise, most worthy of my worthy knights!
There is no man more suited to keep order.
Precision, efficiency, obedience
are the recipe for making men fight to their deaths.

PRINCE:
Clearly, no man is more
precisely blah blah blah!

MALVOLIO:
Pardon me?

KING:
He speaks nonsense. Like he always does.

PRINCE:
Nonsense or no,
I'll be king one day.
Then, I'll show my generosity too.
Give you a dukedom, anything you desire.
You may kiss my ring.
Can I go now, Father?

KING:
But it will be a while yet,
before you're giving out dukedoms.
I'm still the dukedom-giver in this kingdom
And I say
I've still got life in me, Son.
Sir, there is a secret I want to tell you.
I am considering the Barbarians' offer of truce.

MALVOLIO:
Your Highness means to surrender?

KING:
I mean to consider giving up a bit of territory. One
territory, actually.
All they ask is that we surrender Illyria.

MALVOLIO: *(Aside)*
My hometown? The place of my torment? The place of
my birth?

PRINCE:
Father, Illyria has many fresh water wells, lakes, and
streams.
And we are living in a time of drought.
I daresay it wouldn't be wise.

KING:
What is your opinion, Brave Knight?

MALVOLIO:
Your Highness, I agree with your son.
Give the landlocked Barbarians our island with its
waterways,
It might make them unstoppable.

PRINCE:
And, more importantly, Illyria is supposed to be mine!
Not an inch of my territory shall we surrender!

KING:
Then we will always be at war, Idiot!

PRINCE:
Drink some more ale, Father.

KING:
Ingrate! Seed of mine that can never be the oak that I
am!
You don't tell me to drink.
I drink when I want to drink.
(He drinks.)

Speaking of Illyria,
There is a strange messenger that has come calling.
My men said I would want to see this one for myself.
They hint I'll find the manner of the message amusing.
Send in the messenger from Illyria!

(VOLINA *enters with* VALENTIN. VOLINA *is dressed like a*
man. Unfortunately, her disguise is not very good. She looks
very much like a girl.)

VALENTIN:
O, King. This personage calls itself Lozizo.
Lozizo claims to have a message for Your Highness
worth hearing.
We thought you might enjoy an introduction to Lozizo.

KING:
Welcome, Lozizo.
You say you are a messenger from Illyria?

VOLINA:
I say it and I am it.

KING:
What is your message?

VOLINA:
A secret one.
I was instructed to speak to Your Highness alone.

PRINCE:
Oh, Father? Can I deal with this? What fun!

KING:
Shut up, son.
Is what you have to say more sacred than maidenhead?

VOLINA:
Yes. No. Perhaps?
In truth, I would be lying if I said I understood what
that meant.

PRINCE:
So would we.

KING:
Never mind. Speak your secret words.
You are among men I completely trust.
Sir, um, well, this man and my son.

VOLINA:
I will take out a dagger and cut my throat
unless Your Highness lets me speak alone with Your
Highness.

MALVOLIO:
Zounds!

KING:
If you must slit your throat,
would you not do us the favor of doing it outside?
Or tell us what you came to say.

PRINCE:
Yes, tell us.

VOLINA:
Fine. I will say all.
I will spare nothing.
Sir Toby Belch…

MALVOLIO: (*Aside*)
That name I have not heard in twenty years,
though the hatred I have of him is as fresh
as the last time he stood before me.

VOLINA:
He harms people. He hurts people. He…

KING:
Out with it, Sirrah!

VOLINA:
He drinks ale!

KING:
I drink ale.
I love ale.
What is wrong with those who drink ale?

VOLINA:
But, ale is supposed to only be used by medics and for
soldiers,
to ease their suffering,
according to Your Highness' decree.

KING:
Those rules are for common men.
How long do you think this crown would stay
upon this head if I enforced the outlawing of ale
among the nobles?
You were wrong to come here.

VOLINA:
I was. I am sorry.

KING:
You will be sorrier still.
I like Sir Toby.
He was a jolly soul in his youth,
more jest in him than my court jester.

VOLINA:
He is criminal in nature.
There's no cruder man than he.

PRINCE:
Father, Father, can I have her?

KING:
No, Son.

(The KING walks around her, taking VOLINA in. Then, he
knocks off her hat. Her long hair is revealed.)

KING:
Maiden, the lying you have done

is not the kind
you should do with your King.

PRINCE:
Yes, that's right.

KING:
Shut up, son.
She's not for you.
I'll let our newly knighted knight
decide your punishment.

MALVOLIO:
Your Highness, I hardly think it is befitting—

VOLINA:
I am Duchess Volina, the daughter of Orsino and Viola.
I demand to be sent home to Illyria immediately.

(The KING *and the* PRINCE *laugh.)*

KING:
You see, Brave Knight, I give you royalty.

PRINCE:
How dare you pretend to be my betrothed?

VOLINA:
Your betrothed?

KING:
Come along, Son.
Knight, enjoy your night
before your return to the battlefield!
Don't ever say your King never gave you nothing!

(The KING *and* PRINCE *exit, leaving* MALVOLIO *and*
VOLINA *alone onstage.)*

VOLINA: *(Aside)*
Everything I've been taught I must unlearn.
Maybe we are more Barbaric than those we call
Barbarians.
If our king is so unjust, maybe there is no justice.

If this war is not righteous, maybe no war is.
It's just games kings play against other kings.
If you're not a king, you're only a—

(MALVOLIO *takes a step towards* VOLINA.)

MALVOLIO:
Lady?

VOLINA:
Do you mean to harm me?

MALVOLIO:
No. But, I want to know who you really are.

VOLINA:
Do not ask who I am!
Ask who I want to be.
I want to be a sword to smite the unjust.
A thorn in their side
Or at least a rock in their shoe.
Instead, I am just a girl from Illyria,
who can't even tell her friends from her enemies.

MALVOLIO:
You are familiar to me.

VOLINA:
Here we go.
Do you mean to harm me?

MALVOLIO:
No. I have sworn to always defend a lady.
I believe you when you say that
you are the daughter of Orsino and Viola.
I knew them long ago.
I was once a steward to your aunt, Olivia.
Tell me, have you ever heard the name of Malvolio?

VOLINA:
No.

MALVOLIO:
I'm not a source of jest in your household?

VOLINA:
No.

MALVOLIO:
How awful. I had thought that remembrance of
my folly would be infamous.
that the wind itself would whisper
Malvolio is to be scorned! Malvolio is to be scorned!

VOLINA:
Winds don't really whisper.

MALVOLIO:
You know, I am somewhat miffed I have been
forgotten.
To be registered as a fool is somehow better
than to not be registered at all.

VOLINA:
Tell me, did you know my mother
when she disguised herself as a boy?
And went by the name of Cesario?

MALVOLIO:
Yes.

VOLINA:
My mother was able to pass as a boy.
Why not I?

MALVOLIO:
You're, well, more…
Never mind.
I will have you sent home tonight safely
with a trusted servant of mine as your guide.

VOLINA:
Now?

MALVOLIO:
Yes. But, before you go, tell me.
Why do you hate Toby?

VOLINA:
Do you know Toby?

MALVOLIO:
Yes, which means I was wronged by him.
There is no man he knows
that he has not wronged.
I would venture to say no woman either.
To hate the hateful is righteous.

VOLINA:
To hate the hateful is to be awake to injustice.

MALVOLIO:
To hate the hateful is a form of loving everything
deserving of honor.

VOLINA:
Nobility.

MALVOLIO:
Protection.

VOLINA:
Grace.

MALVOLIO:
Valor.

VOLINA:
Passion.

MALVOLIO:
Dignity.

VOLINA:
Love!
Sir, I appreciate you.

MALVOLIO:
Oh. Um. Thank you?
I appreciate you, too.

VOLINA:
I'm not being clear.
I appreciate you
in every way a man can be appreciated.
I know you were not born great.

MALVOLIO:
You speak of my station in life? My class?

VOLINA:
Only to say money and titles mean nothing to me.

MALVOLIO:
Wait here. I'll send for your guide.

VOLINA:
But, Sir—

MALVOLIO:
Good night.
(*He exits.*)

VOLINA:
Good night. Dear Malvolio,
it is a good night.
For I have met the one I want to wish
me good night every night.
Define a man not only by what he does
but what he doesn't,
when the mute moon is the only witness,
when there's no consequences
for acting less than gracious.
Soldier,
you had the chance to hurt me,
but you chose not to.
Were I a man and could take what I wanted,
would I be like you?

Malvolio!
Will not the echo
of my calling your name in the night
outlast you and me
and all that are here
to hear it?

Are you as proud, proper, gentlemanly as you seem?
Can any man be?
Whatever you are,
you are the man for me.

Scene 4

(Entrance of ORSINO's *house.* MARIA *is onstage.* VOLINA
enters with CURIOUS *in tow.)*

VOLINA:
I daresay, you may leave me here.

CURIOUS:
Master Malvolio asked me to ensure your safety.
I'm to deliver you directly to your parents.

VOLINA:
Can you tell this gentleman I reside here?

MARIA:
She belongs to this house.

CURIOUS:
Are you her mother?

MARIA:
I'm married to a cousin of her aunt by marriage, once
removed.

CURIOUS:
Close enough.
(He exits.)

VOLINA:
Maria, I know you to be a clever woman.
Do not tell my parents of this
and I will reward you.

MARIA:
With money?
You think I need money from a baby.

VOLINA:
Yes.

MARIA:
You are right.
I married Toby because I thought
it would be fine to marry a nobleman.
But a nobleman without a coin cannot stay noble very
long.
Nor can his wife.
Fifty ducats?

VOLINA:
Fine.
How is it that you stay married to that man?

MARIA:
What can I do?
He's my husband.
When you wed,
you will forgive and forget
the unforgivable and the unforgettable too.

VOLINA:
Not I, Aunt Maria. Not I.

MARIA:
Just wait. Where are you coming from?

VOLINA:
It doesn't matter.
All that matters is I met a great man.
A wonderful man.

A man better than any other man from Illyria.
Kind. Courteous. Dignified.

(Enter TOBY. *He is drunk.)*

TOBY:
Maria! Damn it! Where'd you run off to? I'm hungry!
Well! Hello, Volina!

VOLINA:
Good-bye!

*(*VOLINA *exits.* TOBY *watches her go.)*

TOBY:
The young duchess is surely a sight for sore eyes.

MARIA:
You're going to have more than sore eyes,
if Orsino ever catches you looking at his daughter like
that.
But I catch you,
you're really going to catch it.
Karma's a female dog, Husband.

TOBY:
Woof!

MARIA:
Don't play!

TOBY:
Woof! Woof!

MARIA:
Watch yourself.

Scene 5

(The PRINCE *stands over the bed of the* KING. MALVOLIO
enters.)

PRINCE:
Malvolio, thank heavens you are here.

MALVOLIO:
I came as soon as I heard.

PRINCE:
I need you by my side.
He drank a great deal of ale.

MALVOLIO:
But, soon his body will purge it, no?

PRINCE:
Then, he fell down an empty well.

MALVOLIO:
But, he appears all right and sound.

PRINCE:
He was, but then the doctors were checking him.
They meant to give him a medicine,
but got their herbs mixed up.
They gave him arsenic instead.
An accident! It's too horrible for words.
The doctors say he may not wake from it
before they ran away,
fearing my wrath.
Look, he stirs.
There is life in him yet.
I do so hope he will recover.
I wanted to be a king without losing a king.

MALVOLIO:
That's generally not possible.

(The KING *wakes up suddenly.)*

KING:
Bring me the freckled one!

PRINCE:
What freckled one, Father?

KING:
What are you taking about?

PRINCE:
You mentioned a—

KING:
I must have been dreaming.
Oh, it's you.

MALVOLIO:
Yes, Your Highness?

KING:
I am not feeling well.

MALVOLIO:
I am sorry for that, Your Highness.

KING:
I've had so many unfortunate accidents
in the past few days.
But. Oh!
(He falls asleep. He stays so still it appears he might have died.)

PRINCE:
He sleeps again.
Perchance to dream. Forever!
Are you dead, my poor father?
Have you left us so soon?
And with no instructions on how to bury you?

(The KING *wakes suddenly again.)*

KING:
I just want to say—

PRINCE:
What now?

KING:
These are words based on my extensive life experience.

PRINCE:
Speak your words.

KING:
These are words that can come
only from having one foot
in this world and one foot in the next.

MALVOLIO:
Tell us, O Master.

KING:
Now that the whirlwind of my days have spun
their last turn,
I finally know.
The process of dying is unpleasant.

PRINCE:
But we already know that.
Tell us.
Father, do you want to be buried in the salmon or
fuchsia-colored robe?

KING:
I'm dying. Do you understand?
Dying!

PRINCE:
And that means what?

KING:
It means I am busy at the moment. You figure the
details out yourself. But I look fabulous in fuchsia.
(*He goes back to sleep.*)

PRINCE:
This is taking longer than I thought.

MALVOLIO:
His recovery?

PRINCE:
Yes, of course. I meant that.
Now, I must drive out these Barbarians.
Send them back to their lands packing,
defeated, erased, remnants of a race.

MALVOLIO:
How do you propose to do it?

PRINCE:
It's simple. I'll put you in charge.
But, unlike my father, I'll give you
the provisions you need to finally win this war.

MALVOLIO:
Okay.

PRINCE:
That means go. Kick some Barbarians back to Barbaria.
I'll be in the brothel if you need me.

Scene 6

(VOLINA's chamber. She is composing a letter.)

VOLINA:
Dearest Malvolio,
You're very handsome.
Mal, be my pal
in the bedroom.
No, that's not right.

How to write the perfect love letter?
How to begin?
Why, one must start somehow
with a single letter,
which must be followed by another and another.
Letters that make up words that make up letters

etched in ink
must be a spell of magic.
Words uttered aloud can be misheard.
But, letters that make up words that make up letters,
which are read in the soft moonlight
stay the same in the unforgiving glare of the sun.
So, here I will make my love known
in the best way that I can.
Letter by letter,
I'll make up a love letter
that will bring my Malvolio to me.
Valentin!

VALENTIN:
You called, my lady?

VOLINA:
Yes! Go the battlefield.
Get this letter to Malvolio.
Take pains to keep it secret.
None other than Malvolio
should see it.

VALENTIN:
I will, my lady.

(NURSE *enters.*)

NURSE:
Child, where have you been?
You disappeared the night of your party.
I saw that your mother's disguise was gone.
And I knew that you were out.
I was so afraid your parents would ask me about you.

VOLINA:
But they did not?

NURSE:
It appears the party tired them out.

VOLINA:
For three whole days?

NURSE:
It was quite a party.
At any rate, I hid your absence.
It never does well for a nurse
to hide the absence of a girl.

VOLINA:
Because they pay you and I do not?

NURSE:
No! Because the world outside is full of ugly things,
and you may come to harm.

VOLINA:
Tell me, is it true that I am betrothed to the prince?

NURSE:
Well, I overheard a maid saying
that she overheard a steward saying
that he overheard your father saying you were
promised to him.

VOLINA:
I will never marry the horrid Prince.
I will run away first,
I love a soldier and he was kind to me.
I have written him the most wonderful letter
and I'm sure he'll soon write back.

Scene 7

(MALVOLIO *opens the letter that the* GUARD *hands him.*)

MALVOLIO:
Dear Malvolio,
I really, really, really love you.
In short, today the alphabet is no more!
We need only

M for the man for whom I have a lifelong plan.
A for my heart's ambition only he can bring into
fruition.
L is for the longing for liberation from you know what.
V is for very unladylike feelings of a lady
What O is for needs no explanation.
What L is for has already been mentioned before.
I is for the I that I'll be, when 'you and me' are 'we.'
O is for only stepping on paths that lead us closer!
Closer! Closer!
Then, closer still! Only when you've merged with me
will I chill.

Abandon your post!
Accost my father. Demand my hand.

If the door is barred, call my name!
Shout it! Coo!
I'll transform into a dove and fly to you.
Then I'll hopefully turn myself back into a lady,
because you'd probably prefer that I do.

Warrior, fight all! Fight everything everywhere,
save passion. Surrender to it, soldier.
Surrender to me.

Love always and love everywhere,
Volina
Postscript. I didn't know before that I like men in
uniform
But apparently I do.
And the man in uniform I like is you.
Yellow is my favorite color!

She mocks me!
Or maybe it is not even she who wrote this?
I have a feeling Sir Toby and his gang might be up to
their old tricks.
Could it be Maria sending me another forged letter?
I will not be prey to such a prank again.
I'll die first.

(MALVOLIO *puts down the letter and the lights shift. The sound of drumming strikes up suddenly. He addresses his men.*)

MALVOLIO:
Brothers, the time has come for our next battle
against the Barbarians.
War is a whore,
We pay her price.
She demands blood money,
in souls—
not coins—
and counts her change in maims.
We pay her price.

If you stay to wage this war with me,
fight the right battle.
—the one raging within yourself—
the battle between who you are
and who you want to be.

(The drumming strikes up again.)

Scene 8

(VIOLA *enters into* VOLINA's *chamber.*)

VIOLA:
Daughter, I'm looking for something.

VOLINA:
My father? He always seems to go missing.

VIOLA:
No, an outfit I used to wear,
when I met your father.
He likes me to wear it now and then.

VOLINA:
What do you mean, Mother?

VIOLA:
He likes me in it, okay?
After our wedding, on our wedding night,
he asked me if I could change into it, okay?
He met me when I was dressed like a boy,
He likes me more when I dress how he met me, okay?
It's a thing he likes.

VOLINA:
I don't even want to think about that, okay?

VIOLA:
Can I give you advice, Daughter?
When a man speaks, listen.
Not to what you want him to say,
but what he actually does.

VOLINA:
What do you mean?

VIOLA:
He told me, men are more infirm
in their affections,
meaning men are fickle.
He was right.

VOLINA:
Mother.

VIOLA:
Yes?

VOLINA:
I do not wish to marry the Prince.

VIOLA:
You have not met him.

VOLINA:
Perhaps I have.

VIOLA:
How?

VOLINA:
In a dream.
He was cruel and crude and vulgar.
What if I don't like him when I meet him?

VIOLA:
Then, let him like you more than you like him.
Daughter, between two lovers, there is one fact.
There is always one who loves the other less.
Be the one who loves less.
Your whole life will be blessed.

VOLINA:
I don't agree, Mother.

ORSINO: *(Off-stage)*
Wife! Wife!

VIOLA:
Coming.
*(She makes to leave, but returns to grab the "Cesario"
costume and exits.)*

Scene 9

(An Illyrian street. TOBY *is in a wheelchair.)*

TOBY:
No cake and ale.
No cake and ale.
And barely any bread.
And barely any bread.
War is murder on a man's stomach.

MARIA:
It's usually murder on more than a man's stomach
if the man joins the war effort and becomes a solider.

TOBY:
I'm unable to fight.

MARIA:
Get up, Toby! Everyone knows you can walk!

(TOBY *stands up.*)

TOBY:
I'm a foul man.

MARIA:
None fouler. But I love you.

TOBY:
You love my title.

MARIA:
It's true. You lifted me up from being a countess's maid
to her cousin.

TOBY:
But I'm starving you nevertheless.
I want to make it up to you somehow.
You see, Maria.
I'm a bad man and I'm having bad thoughts.

MARIA:
I'm ready for you, Toby.
It's been so long.

TOBY:
Not those kinds of thoughts.
You know I had friends among the Barbarians.

MARIA:
Yes?

TOBY:
I have an idea.

MARIA:
Yes?

TOBY:
It's treasonous in nature.

MARIA:
Everything fun is treasonous in nature.

TOBY:
Water is as precious as gold to the landlocked
Barbarian nation.
I'll fill a barge with barrels of water,
have the Barbarians I know from the enemy camp
meet us in the middle of the salty sea.
And exchange our water for their money.
But, I can't do it alone.
I'm no sailor.

MARIA:
I know how to row.

TOBY:
No. I need to get a seafaring man involved,
a man like Sebastian.

MARIA:
But Sebastian is dead.

TOBY:
That's what we heard, but it's not true.
Sebastian found marriage to Olivia tiresome.
You know, they barely knew each other when they
wed.
So he took a great deal of her money
And pretended he was going out to sea.
Instead, Sebastian is hiding out here in Illyria,
living in the brothel.

MARIA:
Do I want to ask how you know who's living at the
brothel?

TOBY:
No.

Scene 10

(The brothel. SEBASTIAN is seated alone, perhaps playing Solitaire. There is a knock at the door. It startles him, before he can react further, TOBY enters.)

TOBY:
Count Sebastian!

SEBASTIAN:
Quieter, Toby. And don't speak my name out loud.

TOBY:
How are you?

SEBASTIAN:
I don't feel like I count at all.

TOBY:
Why not?

SEBASTIAN:
I'm running out of money.
The madam won't keep me here,
unless I continue to pay her.

TOBY:
Good to hear.

SEBASTIAN:
Why is that good to hear?

TOBY:
Because I have a proposition for you.
A lucrative one.
Some friends of mine need water.
There's money to be made in supplying it.

SEBASTIAN:
Are these friends of yours friendly to our King?

TOBY:
Of course!
Our King is just.

That means, he's a friend to all.
It's blasphemy to say otherwise.
Meet me under the bridge at midnight.
I'll have the boat ready. I just need you to captain it.

SEBASTIAN:
I can't.

TOBY:
Why?

SEBASTIAN:
Why do you think I haven't left this deathtrap of an
island yet?

TOBY:
Perhaps because you enjoy the pleasures of this place?

SEBASTIAN:
You've got me wrong, Toby.
I'm living here. Nothing more.
These women are my friends.
I've never had women in my life who were just friends.
When I stopped just looking at them
and started listening to them,
I learned.
It's hard being a woman.

TOBY:
Hardly! Women don't even have to go to war.

SEBASTIAN:
Women are always at war,
the minute they step out their door.
Can never anticipate when next
they'll be attacked without warning.
No one asks what kind of day they're having
when one of us men are catcalling them.
Following them down alleys.
feeling them up in crowds.
Or worse.

TOBY:
And no one cares.

SEBASTIAN:
Exactly. No one cares!
It's a wonder not more women are mad.
It's a wonder not more men are dead.
But, once I chose to flee Olivia, what other choice did I have,
except to hole up and hide out here?
I'm stuck in Illyria.
Last time I sailed,
I almost drowned.
I'm afraid of being out on the open seas now.

TOBY:
Friend, you must face your fear.
What are you going to do?
You can't hide out in a brothel forever.

Scene 11

(The battle camp)

CURIOUS:
Sir, the prince calls for you.

MALVOLIO:
Has the king died?

CURIOUS:
Not yet.

(The lights shift. MALVOLIO *enters the royal chamber where the* PRINCE *is waiting.)*

PRINCE:
Greetings, Sir Malvolio.
What news do you have for us of the war?

MALVOLIO:
I'm sure if they are not fortified with more supplies
the Barbarians will surely fall.

PRINCE:
Good tidings!

MALVOLIO:
Not really. There are many traitors amongst your
subjects
who would trade with our enemies to line their
pockets.

PRINCE:
Don't I know it?
Few are as loyal as you have proved yourself,
time and time again, to be to my father.
And I hope—one day—you will be to me.
If, I mean, when you survive the war
and are victorious, I will grant you one wish.
Mind you, make it reasonable.
I am no genie. I'm just a king,
But any position in my kingdom you want,
you will have.

MALVOLIO:
Will you make me your representative in Illyria?

PRINCE:
So that all the people there will have to bend their knee
to you?
As you wish, Malvolio.
But Illyria's not the richest island in my realm.

MALVOLIO:
It is what I ask.

PRINCE:
Then, Illyria will be yours.
Go and let God go with you.

(MALVOLIO *exits.*)

VALENTIN:
You know he'll never win that battle.
You will have to cede some territory to the Barbarians.

PRINCE:
If any man can win this for us, it is he.
There is no man more disciplined, brave, or boring.
I don't understand why he is so keen on being
stationed in Illyria.
It's a small island.

VALENTIN:
It's not small to him.
He's lowborn.
He was once a lowly steward to the Countess Olivia.

PRINCE:
Olivia. I haven't heard that name in years.
I used to call her Countess Coldcut.
She was the coldest piece of meat I ever met.
She never would flirt with me!
I, who was one day going to be her King!
If this Volina—who I am betrothed to—is not of my
liking—
I will take Olivia and force her to wed me.

VALENTIN:
There are rumors about Olivia's household
involving Malvolio.
It is said that Malvolio suffered some grave humiliation
at the hands of Olivia's kinsman, Sir Toby Belch,
and her fool.
He swore revenge.

PRINCE:
But, revenge he will not likely get.
I don't think his Legion of the Cross Gartered will get
very far.
Let him fight one more battle,

but I know this war is likely to never end
until I give up land.

(The lights shift. VALENTIN *approaches* MALVOLIO.)

VALENTIN:
Sir Malvolio, I have a message for you
from Illyria.

*(*VALETIN *hands* MALVOLIO *a letter.* VALETIN *exits.)*

MALVOLIO:
Not another letter from that girl, Volina!
Or from someone who is pretending to write me
in her hand in order to mock me!

No, it is from my mother.

Dear Son,

I hear news of you, but you never write.
Why is a mother's love so taken for granted?

To every mother, her son is a prince.
I am no exception.
You were destined for a higher life
than the one I could give you,
but fate wanted it otherwise.

Don't be an idiot.
Keep yourself safe.
Whoever said
"Hell hath no fury like a woman scorned"
never met a woman who buried a child she's born.
Spare me such fury.
Spare our world.
Because if a Barbarian takes you from me,
I may not get revenge upon every one of their heads,
but I will die trying.

When in my belly, you kicked.
Food I could not keep nor barely walk due to the
weight of you.
But I was infinitely more comfortable then,

when within my folds you were immersed.
Knowing to get at you, the world had to go through
me first.
Stay alive.
Love,
Mom

Scene 12

(TOBY *and* SEBASTIAN *enter. They are on a dock.*)

SEBASTIAN:
Toby, I'm not so sure I'm up to the task.

TOBY:
Nonsense.

(FOOL *enters.*)

FOOL:
Greetings!

SEBASTIAN:
What is he doing here?

TOBY:
We needed an extra pair of hands.

SEBASTIAN:
I thought we were working alone, Toby.
No one is supposed to know I'm still alive.

FOOL:
Worry not. I will guard your secret with my life.
But, then again I am a fool.
It might slip out.

SEBASTIAN:
I really am not ready to return to sea.

FOOL:
But you must, cuckold.

SEBASTIAN:
Excuse me?

TOBY:
Oh, shut your trap!
Hurry!
See that boat in the distance,
coming our way.
It's the men I've arranged for us to meet
in the middle of the sea.
Quickly, let's board.

SEBASTIAN:
I'm afraid.
I felt a drop of rain on my forehead.
A storm is surely brewing.

TOBY:
What are you talking about?
There hasn't been a clearer night ever.
It's going to be smooth sailing for us.

SEBASTIAN:
You're right.

(They board a boat and start rowing.)

SEBASTIAN:
Oh, no! That's not another boat!
It's a whale. We are drowned!

(They exit, pursued by a whale.)

Scene 13

(The lights shift to reveal TOBY, SEBASTIAN, *and* FOOL *as
they wash up on a shore. They look wet and exhausted.)*

SEBASTIAN:
What country, fool, is this?

FOOL:
How should I know? I just landed here too.

(CURIOUS *enters.*)

CURIOUS:
No one move!

TOBY:
I couldn't if I tried.

CURIOUS:
What are you doing here?

TOBY:
I was just taking a little spin on my boat.

CURIOUS:
During wartime?

TOBY:
Yes. Just because it is wartime,
do you think there should be no spinning on boats?

CURIOUS:
In enemy territory? With provisions?
With water?

SEBASTIAN:
Is that what you had us doing, Toby?

TOBY:
Of course not!
Sir, we are patriots from Illyria,
coming here in order to, um,
to fortify you!
These are gifts of provisions to our dear soldiers.
It's the least we felt we could do.

CURIOUS:
Really?
Let's see if our commander believes your story,
for I do not.

(MALVOLIO *appears.*)

CURIOUS:
Sir Malvolio, these shipwrecked men were heading
into enemy seas.

TOBY:
Sir Malvolio! You are their commander?

MALVOLIO:
Yes, I am, Sir Toby Belch!

CURIOUS:
I do not know if these men are your friends.
But I daresay they were trading with the Barbarians.
Their boat was full of barrels of fresh water.

MALVOLIO:
When the enemy battlecamps are plagued by drought?
You know I swore revenge upon you, Toby!

TOBY:
You can't still be upset about that little, little prank we
played upon you.

SEBASTIAN:
I played no prank upon anyone.
I'm no prankster.

MALVOLIO:
Just a traitor.
fortifying the troops of the enemies.

SEBASTIAN:
We deserve your wrath, Sir.

TOBY:
No, we don't.
We really don't.
Malvolio, may you give me leave to speak?

MALVOLIO:
There's nothing you can say.
Fool me once, shame on you.
Fool me twice, shame on—

(*Enter the* PRINCE.)

PRINCE:
Malvolio, what is happening?
Who are these men?

MALVOLIO:
Enemies of your state.
These perfidious men from Illyria are selling
provisions to the Barbarians,
which has been prolonging the war against your
kingdom.

PRINCE:
Well, that's not very nice.
Should we cut off their heads?
Hang them?
Have them drawn and quartered?
Burned at the stake?

MALVOLIO:
These are no ordinary traitors.
You see, I hate these men for personal reasons.
They were my enemies from long ago.

PRINCE:
So, basically, you want to prolong their torture?

MALVOLIO:
Something like that.
Will you leave them to me?

TOBY:
Fair Prince, your father and I were once great friends.

FOOL:
And I was one of his favorite fools.

PRINCE:
Well, that's good to know,
since I happen to hate my father.
You know I can't deny you anything, Malvolio.
Torture these men any way you like,

pop out their eyes,
dig out their hearts!
Or better yet,
Do you like cricket?

MALVOLIO:
Sure.

PRINCE:
I'll provide the bat mallets.
Why don't you secure us some balls?

(SEBASTIAN, FOOL, *and* TOBY *cover themselves.*)

PRINCE:
Call me when it's game time.
I'm going to check on my father.
(He exits.)

TOBY:
Please! Please!
Have mercy.

MALVOLIO:
Toby, Toby, Toby.
I must be round with you.
I've been dreaming of this moment,
for so long
have I longed for you
to lay prostrate before me,
begging for mercy.
And here it is!

TOBY:
Spare me!
For the sake of my poor children!

MALVOLIO:
You have children, Toby?

TOBY:
Not really. Not yet! But I might! Have mercy!

FOOL:
Do what you will. Take my balls, but kill me first.

MALVOLIO:
Yes, um, great.
Glad you see it my way.
May we hold that thought for a moment?
I'm a bit stumped right now about what to do first,
though I warn you,
I will have vengeance!
It will be very, very, very vengeful!
The most vengeful vengeance the world ever did see.

TOBY, FOOL & SEBASTIAN:
No! PLEASE!!!

MALVOLIO:
Will you three wait here?
I mean, none of you move!
(Aside)
I've never made a decision of this magnitude.
Let me consult with my legion of men.
(He addresses CURIOUS.*)*
What day is this, sirrah?

CURIOUS:
It is the Thirteenth Day!
Or is the Twelfth?
No, it the Thirteenth, I'm sure.

MALVOLIO:
Mark it as a blessed day.
For I am able to avenge the men
who so long ago tormented me.
Assemble the Legion before me.
(He addresses his men.)
Legion of the Cross-Gartered.
Battalion of the Bravest of our Brave King's Men.
Brothers, I—who have long led you—need now to be
led.

Long ago I was a steward to a countess,
a beautiful woman named Olivia.
One of her kinsmen and her fool noticed I loved that
countess.
They played an evil trick on me,
sent me love letters
that were sealed with my lady's seal.

They fooled me into thinking my lady
was confessing her passion for me.

But was that enough? No.

Why do I have you dress in cross-gartered yellow
stockings?
Their false letters instructed me to wear the style my
lady found most unbecoming.
So, she might be offended by the very sight of me.
And, like a badge of courage, I—and you men who
follow me—
now wear it evermore.

But was that enough? No.

They imprisoned me in a small dark room.
And swore it was full of light.
Tried to make me mistrust my very senses.

But, surely, that was enough? No.
They exposed my folly for all the world to see.
I swore revenge.

Now, I've caught them in an act of great treason.
I—who has always orchestrated the battles you fight—
must ask your advice.
What punishment fits their crime?

SERVANT #1:
It is hard to know.

MALVOLIO:
I know, right?
You, Sir, speak first and tell me.

What's happened to you to make you bitter?
And what did you do about it?

SERVANT #1:
My uncle killed my father and married my mother.

MALVOLIO:
Zounds. That is a crime of intensity
that I must say surpasses mine.

SOLDIER #2:
A man in my army decided to convince me
my wife was unfaithful.

MALVOLIO:
And what did you do about it?

SOLDIER #2:
Well, I killed my wife,
though she was faithful to me.

MALVOLIO:
That wasn't too clever of you.

SOLDIER #3:
My daughter was raped
and the rapist cut off her tongue and hands
so she could never tell—
or write down—
who raped her.

MALVOLIO:
Okay, I can't even fathom that.
Obviously, you all suffered a bit more than I did.
This is not helping!

Scene 14

(PRINCE *enters the room of the* KING, *who looks dead.*)

PRINCE:
Oh, Father. There you are. Dead.

KING:
Hello, Son.

PRINCE:
Zounds. What happened?

KING:
Well, I'm not sure, but I didn't die.

PRINCE:
I had you knocked down a long well,
and you lived.
Then, I had you poisoned.
And you still talk and walk and breathe!

KING:
What? I'm your father!
How could you kill me?!

PRINCE:
I haven't killed you,
I've only tried.

KING:
Well, how could you try?
I'm your father.

PRINCE:
You always treat me like I'm a failure.

KING:
Do you blame me?
You can't even succeed in killing an old man.

PRINCE:
It's hard. I have to make it look like an accident.
Do you know how challenging that is?

KING:
I do. Look, Son.
I wanted to kill my father.
Of course, I didn't attempt it,
But I understand the feeling.

PRINCE:
So are you not going to punish me?

KING:
Of course.
I'm going to make you get married.
I'll send word to noble Orsino
that we'll soon be asking for his daughter's hand.

PRINCE:
That's all?

KING:
You think getting married is no punishment,
because you've never done it.
I have no other heir.
No other son.
What can I do?
Honestly, what can I do,
except get myself a few more guards to protect me
from you?
No punishment ever fits the crime.
I'll tell Orsino that his daughter, the fair Volina,
is to ready herself to be your bride.

PRINCE:
Does it have to be Volina?
I had feelings for the Countess Olivia.
If Volina is not of my liking,
may I marry Olivia?

KING:
But Olivia is older than you.
Maybe too old to bear children.
And that's all I ask of you.

PRINCE:
I've always wanted to teach Countess Coldcut
a thing or two.

KING:
Give me a grandchild!
Give me some line of descendants beneath me
that includes someone other than you.

PRINCE:
Fine! Fine. I'll marry Volina.

Scene 15

(VOLINA's *chamber*)

VOLINA:
The Prince wants to marry me.
How awful. How horrid.
How wrong!
I am in love with another man.
Should I jump from my balcony?
That would be scary.
I could try to drown myself.
But, I know how to swim.
I could waste away,
But I like pulled pork too much.
My tragedy is I'm not tragic enough.
Mother! Father!

(*Enter* ORSINO *and* VIOLA.)

VOLINA:
Please don't make me marry him.
Please cancel the wedding!

ORSINO:
Can't.
The marriage is being arranged by the king.
To refuse his request would be treason.
And, what's more,
the wedding banquet has already been planned.

We've ordered lobster
for hundreds of guests.

VIOLA:
What would we do with the lobster?

VOLINA:
I don't care.

ORSINO:
Do you know how expensive lobster is?

VOLINA:
Father!

ORSINO:
Not another word!

Scene 16

(MALVOLIO *and* CURIOUS *are onstage.*)

MALVOLIO:
I still don't know
what do I do with Toby and the others?
It seems strange to torture them.
Toby has no shame, so I can't shame him.
He's friendly
so he'll probably eek some joy out of the comradeship
of jail.
What do I do?

CURIOUS:
When you can't make a decision,
there is an art that helps you make it
or at least delay it—
a magic art in which we are all master magicians.

MALVOLIO:
What art is that?

CURIOUS:
The art of procrastination.
The next battle we must fight against the Barbarians
will be bigger than any battle we've fought before.
Why don't you focus on that at the present moment?

MALVOLIO:
You're right.
I'll just keep them jailed until after the battle.

(*Lights up on* TOBY, FOOL *and* SEBASTIAN)

TOBY:
This may be our way out.

SEBASTIAN:
I want no way out.
Sir Malvolio, let me join your legion.
Let me fight by your side.
If I'm killed,
at least I'll spare you the trouble of deciding
what to do with my worthless life.
If a man who has lived like a coward
doesn't want to die a coward,
his only choice is dying bravely.

TOBY:
How about living bravely?
That's an option.
I like that option.

CURIOUS:
But it's not an option open to many during wartime.
We need soldiers.
Let them fight alongside us, Sir Malvolio.
After our battle,
if they live,
I'm sure you will find for them a fitting revenge.

MALVOLIO:
You are right.

VALENTIN:
The King has recovered!
The King has recovered!

(The men cheer.)

MALVOLIO:
This is a good sign.

TOBY: *(Aside)*
A great sign for me.
The King is my great friend.

MALVOLIO:
Men, let's go do battle
and win this war once and for all!
For our king!

(The lights shift. There is drumming. We see the soldiers fighting a battle. This can be staged as a dance or montage of images of the soldiers in red light. SEBASTIAN, TOBY, and FOOL are now dressed in the cross-gartered yellow stocking uniform. In these images, it is clear the SEBASTIAN is distinguishing himself as a valiant soldier while TOBY and FOOL are hiding behind rocks, playing dead, and otherwise not participating fully.)

Scene 17

(Lights up on VOLINA in her chamber.)

VOLINA:
I have not heard from my beloved soldier.
Perchance he did not receive my last letter.
I must write again.
Surely my brave knight will make it
so I don't have to marry the prince.

(Lights up on MALVOLIO, who looks exhausted and is resting after battle.)

CURIOUS:
Congratulations on the great battle, Sir.
Here is a letter for you.

(CURIOUS *hands* MALVOLIO *the letter.*)

MALVOLIO: *(Reading the letter)*
Dear Sir Malvolio,
Hi again.
I wrote you a letter confessing my love.
Urging you to abandon your post.
Break down the door of my father's house.
I was all requests, all demands.
I left all the action in your hands.

You were touchy when I alluded to your station and
your state.
Yes, you are very, very, very poor.
I speak of it only to say
money has no meaning
in a world
that sees a man like you as broke.
If my words somehow offended thee,
you misheard or I misspoke.

Tell me where to meet you.
Give me a time, a place.
The only thing I ask of you is do it in haste.
Your love,
Volina

Postscript.
Myself, I would seriously blame
If I didn't emphasize the tight time frame.
The prince is in his way.
You have about a day.
We ordered lobsters.
(He puts down the letter.)
Could this letter really be from her?
No! Someone is trying to mock me!

Let us go wreak more revenge upon the Barbarian
army.
Let's fight.

CURIOUS:
Sir, that's not the only message I have for you.
I am told I must inform you
that the Barbarians have sent an emissary to our king
to ask for a truce.

MALVOLIO:
What?

CURIOUS:
Didn't you see our enemies fleeing?

MALVOLIO:
Yes, but they always come back!

CURIOUS:
The King calls for you, Sir Malvolio.

Scene 18

(KING *and* PRINCE *are seated.*)

KING:
So, I say the guest list is rather large.

PRINCE:
Father, it's only fitting that we invite all the nobles to
my wedding.

KING:
True, but must we invite the lesser ones?
Of course, we must invite all the counts,
but viscounts as well?

(VALENTIN *enters.*)

VALENTIN:
Your Highness, Sir Malvolio is here.

(MALVOLIO *enters*.)

MALVOLIO:
You called, Your Highness?

KING:
Yes, that war thing.
It's over.

MALVOLIO:
But the Barbarians often go back on their word when
they—

KING:
Over. It's over.
They've surrendered.

PRINCE:
And you must come to my wedding!

KING:
Son, he's hardly worthy.
No commoners!
We went over this.
You invite one of them,
all the rest of their class gets annoyed.
They hold grudges.
Don't want to pay taxes or fight in the next war, Son.
We'd love to have you, but you understand why we
can't invite you.
Right, Brave Knight?

MALVOLIO:
Yes, of course, Your Highness.

KING:
There! That right there is loyalty.
Oh, we like you, Magnolio.

MALVOLIO:
It's Malvolio, Your Highness.
Anyway, I'm not one for banquets.

KING:
You see?! He doesn't even want to come.

PRINCE:
But, Father, he's a war hero!
If the Barbarians do come back,
we'll need soldiers like him,
willing to die for us.

KING:
Fine. Come to the wedding.

MALVOLIO:
I would really rather not.

PRINCE:
See?! You've hurt his pride.

KING:
I forget that commoners sometimes have pride.
Look, you are saying you don't want to come
because you think we don't really want you to come.
You know enough to know
a king doesn't always mean what he says
or says what he means.
That's the fun of being a king!
But we really want you to come.
We won't take no for an answer.

PRINCE:
I'm very excited.
I want my bride.
I'm ready.
My dewy sweet Maiden
I've composed a song I want to sing to her.
It's called "I Want Your Maidenhead".
(Sings)
Heigh, ho! You're in for some pain!
Maiden, head on to the church.
My soft, unbroken Bride.

Peace be upon you!
Because your peace is my peace now.
Oh, Lady!
Cheery I am when I dream of your cherry,
cherry lips.
Your ignorance is my bliss.
For if I'm good or bad in bed,
you won't know it.
That means there is no way for me to blow it.

Bride! Bride! I'm rough. Be ready.
I want my juicy maiden.
Meet me at the altar,
after which you will be altered for good.

KING:
I suggest you don't sing that song to her,
at least not until after the wedding.
I heard Sir Toby and Count Sebastian fought with you.
Is that so?

MALVOLIO:
Yes, Your Highness.

KING:
And that wonderful fool that goes by the name of
Feste?

MALVOLIO:
They were doing it as a penance for treason,
and did not enlist of their own free will.

KING:
Treason? What kind of treason?

MALVOLIO:
They were selling provisions like water to the
Barbarians.

KING:
So?
Noblemen are always looking for ways to make a buck

during wartime.
Who begrudges them that?
They are friends of mine.
You wouldn't dare to suggest we punish my friends.

MALVOLIO:
And they also played pranks upon me
while I was in Illyria.

KING:
Like what?

(Pause)

MALVOLIO:
Never mind.

KING:
Wonderful! Toby and the Fool can ride in the boat with
us to Illyria
in my guest chamber.
None make me laugh like those two.
And you must come also.
I'm sure the deckhands would make a bed for you
In the servants' cabin.

MALVOLIO:
Yes, Your Highness.

Scene 19

*(*TOBY, KING, PRINCE, *and* FOOL *are drinking and reveling
on the deck of a large boat.* MALVOLIO *enters.)*

MALVOLIO:
Here I am aboard a boat to Illyria,
sailing straight towards all I left behind.
Here I am trying to right the world's wrongs.
Your Highness! The servants sent me as an emissary.
They are hungry and wondering when you'll give
them leave to eat.

TOBY: *(Clearly drunk)*
How now? O, General Malvolio,
most general of all generalities!
Soldier of misfortune!
Does not this fellow put the "k" in knave?

FOOL:
I actually think it's nice he didn't cut off our—

TOBY:
Stew on this, Steward!
You must learn your—

(TOBY stumbles and falls overboard. There is a loud splash.)

MALVOLIO:
Zounds! We must stop the boat.
We might save him.

PRINCE:
My bet is he's a goner.

KING:
Yes. Toby died as he wanted to live. Drunk. Happy.
More importantly, we can't be late for my son's
wedding.

MALVOLIO: *(To FOOL)*
What should we do?

FOOL: *(To MALVOLIO)*
What can we do?

KING:
Onwards!

Scene 20

(Orsino's home. VOLINA is dressed in a wedding gown.
NURSE is putting a veil on her.)

NURSE:
It's time we left for the church.

VOLINA:
I feel as if I am going to my funeral, Nurse.

NURSE:
Enough of that.
Many a girl would dream of marrying a crown prince.

VOLINA:
But, I love another.
Nurse, will you not help me run?

NURSE:
I cannot.
I know I do you a kindness by being unkind.
By keeping you where you are supposed to be,
I'm keeping you safe. Maybe even alive.
The last girl I helped run off with her true love
ended up waking up in a tomb
finding her lover dead before her,
and stabbing herself.
You don't want to end up like that.

VOLINA:
Nurse, you know that wouldn't be me.
If I woke up and found my beloved Malvolio—

NURSE:
Did you say Malvolio?

VOLINA:
Yes. Don't tell my parents, but it is he that I love!

NURSE:
The leader of the Legion of the Cross-Gartered?

VOLINA:
Yes, I have offered to run away with him,
but he hasn't answered any of my letters.

NURSE:
If it is Malvolio you want,
then Malvolio you shall get.
That man is my son!

Scene 21

(A church in Illyria. VIOLA *is on-stage.* OLIVIA *enters. They are wearing the same dress.)*

OLIVIA:
You look nice.

VIOLA:
I thought if I ordered the latest style of dress from Dalmatia.
No one would have it here.

OLIVIA:
I thought that too.
Should I go home and change?

VIOLA:
You won't have time.
The Prince and his retinue are on the way.

OLIVIA:
Oh, we look like twins, don't we?

VIOLA:
No.

OLIVIA:
Well, I think we do.
Weddings are so wonderful.
Little Volina,
My goddaughter,
Getting married.
Can you believe it?

VIOLA:
Oh, for a baton of fire
to shove up your—

OLIVIA:
I see you have not forgiven me.
Nor should you.
Since you've made it clear this day is the last we'll ever

speak,
let us speak openly.

(VIOLA *turns to go.*)

OLIVIA:
Wait! It's about your brother.
I was not kind to Sebastian
I treated him with disdain.
I was angry at you,
and lashed out in the way I was sure would hurt you
the most,
in the way women use men to hurt other women
that has nothing to do with men.
You see, I blamed you for my unhappy marriage.
Do not forget when you dressed as a boy
and you were impersonating him,
you spoke such sweet words to me.
When I mistook him for you,
I loved him for your fine words.
No one can woo a woman like a woman.
Who knows best what we most need to hear,
how to make an alchemy of blatant flattery
fuse with delicate promises of impossible fidelity,
than we ourselves?
He couldn't compete.
I think that is why he left me.
He told me he was frightened of the sea,
but I think my coldness
—my rage at him for not being you—
frightened him even more.
How I wish Sebastian were alive and I could make it
up to him!
How I wish I could tell him—
for a man—
you're not bad.
Not bad at all.

VIOLA:
I wish my brother was alive, too.
Goodbye, Olivia.

OLIVIA:
One more thing.
You must care less, Viola.

VIOLA:
What?

OLIVIA:
I've known Orsino since we were children.
Your man was a boy who liked a chase
and he has never grown up.
Care less and I bet he'll care more for you.

VIOLA:
I didn't ask your advice.

OLIVIA:
All I'm saying is try it, Viola.

(ORSINO *enters with* VOLINA, *who is wearing a fabulous wedding dress.* FATHER TOPAS *enters behind them.*)

OLIVIA:
You look wondrous, Volina.

VIOLA:
You are a beautiful bride, Daughter.

ORSINO:
Do I look all right?

VIOLA:
For someone your age and your complexion,
you look adequate.

ORSINO:
Adequate? You've always preferred a man of my
complexion.
In your youth, that's all you'd speak of.

VIOLA:
That was in my youth.
Before I had seen very much.

ORSINO:
Do you fancy someone else, Wife?

VIOLA:
I am always faithful to you, Husband.
And always will be.

ORSINO:
That wasn't my question, Viola.

(A horn is blown.)

VIOLA:
The Prince is coming.
You must leave us now, Daughter.
He must not see you before
you arrive at the altar.

(VOLINA exits before the KING, SEBASTIAN, MALVOLIO, and the FOOL enter.)

KING:
Did someone say they're serving lobsters?

(All bow to the KING.)

ORSINO:
Dear King!
You honor us with your presence.

KING:
I know.

OLIVIA:
Sebastian! You're alive?!

VIOLA:
Brother! Can it be you?

SEBASTIAN:
I was miraculously saved from a shipwreck. Again!

OLIVIA:
Husband, how I'm missed you!

(Both OLIVIA *and* VIOLA *kiss* SEBASTIAN *on the cheeks and hug him.)*

OLIVIA:
But, Sebastian, if you were saved from a shipwreck,
Why didn't you come home?
Where were you?

SEBASTIAN:
Closer than you think.
But, most recently, I went to defend our people.
I fought in the legion of Malvolio's men.
He's here too.

*(*MARIA *enters. She approaches* FOOL.*)*

MARIA:
Where is my husband?

FOOL:
Let's just say Toby was shipwrecked. Permanently.

MARIA:
Do I want to know the details?

FOOL:
No.
But you should know Malvolio tried to save him.

*(*OLIVIA *approaches* MALVOLIO.*)*

OLIVIA:
Malvolio! Is that you?

MALVOLIO:
Yes, my lady.

OLIVIA:
Welcome home.
How does it feel to be back?

MALVOLIO:
It feels—

(SEBASTIAN *motions for* OLIVIA *to join him in another part of the stage. She turns her back on* MALVOLIO, *not bothering to hear his answer to her question.*)

MALVOLIO:
—the same.

KING:
Let's get this marriage on the road.

FOOL:
I, who have recently been ordained,
will do the honor of performing the marriage
ceremony.

(*Music plays as the* PRINCE *and the* FOOL *assemble themselves at the altar.* ORSINO *walks down the aisle with* VOLINA. *The* PRINCE *is startled when he sees* VOLINA.)

PRINCE:
Wait a minute. I know that girl.
Veils are not thick enough to hide the truth.
Stop. We cannot have this marriage, Father.
She's no fresh maiden.
She's the girl who came dressed as a boy
to the battlefield.
You gave her to Malvolio!

KING:
What does it matter?

PRINCE:
I wanted a virgin.

VOLINA:
And it is Malvolio I want.

MALVOLIO: (*Aside*)
If this is a joke,

she seems to be taking it very far.
Could such a lovely lady really love me?

KING:
Marriage isn't about what you want.
It's about fulfilling long-decreed duties to ancestors.
The Crown Prince must marry a noblewoman from
Illyria.

(NURSE *enters and approaches the* KING.)

NURSE:
But what if the Crown Prince is not who you think he
is?

KING:
Can it be you, Bambi?

NURSE:
Yes. It is I.

KING:
But I thought you were dead.
This is my true wife that I married in secret.
She's the daughter of my nurse
that I loved all my life.
My father told me you died, Bambi.

NURSE:
No, he tried to have me killed.
In fact, he ordered this priest who married us in secret
to kill me.
But, Father Topas could not do it.
He brought me to Illyria,
where I bore you a son I called Malvolio.
I have kept the truth of his royal blood secret,
even from him.

KING:
Is that true, Father Topas?

FATHER TOPAS:
Yes, Your Highness.

KING:
So Monrovio is my son?

EVERYONE: *(Except* KING*)*
Malvolio!

KING:
You are my firstborn!
I thought I was a widower
when I married a second time.

PRINCE:
That makes me a bastard!

KING:
A bastard who tried to kill me.
Hang him!

MALVOLIO:
Father, please pardon my half-brother.

KING:
Why?

MALVOLIO:
Because it's my wedding day.
I was apparently born great and did not know it.
So how worthwhile can being born great really be?
Maybe true greatness is only measurable
by the satisfaction a man gets
when he shows forgiveness and mercy.
In short, when he manages to have a sense of humor.
To take a slight with a smile.
To know a mountain from a molehill.

VOLINA:
To find love in a loveless world.
You got my letters, right?

MALVOLIO:
I did.

(MALVOLIO *offers* VOLINA *his hand. She takes it.*)

MALVOLIO:
Unbelievably good fortune is truly the best revenge.
Your ending can be happier
than your wildest scheme
of righting every wrong.

VOLINA:
Only half of luck depends on chance.
The rest of luck rests on you.

MALVOLIO:
Half of luck is knowing you're lucky.
And I'm lucky enough to know
how lucky I am
to have…

VOLINA:
(Aside) Do I even want to get married?
To risk ending up like all the rest?
I, who only knows how to love more. Can't love less.

MALVOLIO:
You.

VOLINA: *(Turning to face* MALVOLIO*)*
Yes.

END OF PLAY

www.ingramcontent.com/pod-product-compliance
Lightning Source LLC
Chambersburg PA
CBHW050800160726
48004CB00002B/645